MOTHERS & OTHER FAIRYTALES

Mothers & Other Fairytales

Rachel J. Bennett

THE WORD WORKS

Author photograph: Alex Vourlidis
Cover art: *Shield with Unicorn, Held by Woman*
(c. 1480) by Martin Schongauer
The National Gallery of Art
Cover design: Susan Pearce

❦

ISBN: 978-1-944585-63-1

Acknowledgments

With gratitude for the encouragement the following journals and their editors provided by publishing versions of these poems:

Five Quarterly: " or   G   o   n   e"
Gigantic Sequins: "Another Thing No One Mentioned About
      Becoming a Mother"
Interim: "Castle"
inter/rupture: "The Mother & the Girl"
LEVELER: "The Girl & the Mother"
Ninth Letter: "Drawbridge"
Poetry Daily: "Floating" (originally published in *Sixth Finch*)
Queen Mob's Teahouse: "On Animals"
Rabbit Catastrophe Review: "Lexicon"
Rattle (Poets Respond): "Unsent Letter from Philae, Comet 67P"
Really System: "Origin Story"
Salt Hill Journal: "Traveler"
Sixth Finch: "The truth is she went missing," "Birdsong," "Level One,"
      "First the Mother," "The Tomboy & the Mother,"
      "The Good-Enough Mother," "Floating"
SplitLevel: "Home Movie"
Sycamore Review: "3D"
Vinyl: "Thinking About Unrequited Love on a Train in Poland"

A few of these poems were originally published in *Game*, a chapbook from dancing girl press. Thank you to Kristy Bowen. One of these, "Level One," was selected for publication in the *Brooklyn Poets Anthology*. Thank you to Jason Koo and Joe Pan.

A thousand thanks to Lynn Melnick and Wynn Cooper for spending time with these poems and helping me along the path. The same to Alex Fong. Thanks to Willa Carroll for her words of encouragement. Gratitude to the 92nd Street Y. For making this book come true, thank you to Nancy White, Susan Pearce, and the team at The Word Works.

Without the particular freedoms and solitudes of New York City, I wouldn't have found my way here. Special gratitude to Steve Andrews, Carol Arnold, Michael Cavanagh, Fred Riccardi, Jean Sommerfield, and my grandparents, Ray and Mabel Bennett. Thanks to Elizabeth Schretzman and Ethan Nichtern for listening and to Leila Ortiz and E. Tammy Kim for our workshops once upon a time. From a time before that, thank you to Dublin. May all who have shown me kindness and friendship over the years know kindness and friendship, wherever you may be.

Our parents are, originally and finally, our parents. Thank you to my mom and those I have looked to. Thank you to my dad for not once failing to show up. Thank you to my brother for keeping Rock Island in the family.

Thanks without end to Alex.

Contents

She went missing   5

❀

The Mother & the Girl   9
Traveler   10
Home Movie   11
Beforetime   12
The Girl & the Mother   13
Birdsong   14
Coat of Arms   16
Thinking About Unrequited Love on a Train in Poland   18
Mother-Daughter   20
Mothers in *The Haunting of Hill House*   21
Level One   22
First the Mother   23
Violence & Magic   23
3D   24

❀

Unsent Letter from Philae, Comet 67P   29
Rome   30
To the Body Inside My Body   31
On Animals   32
Lexicon   33
Reverie   34
The Tomboy & the Mother   36
As If You Could Expect Anything at All   37
Those Months You Were Afloat   39
Castle   40
Upon a Time   41
Drawbridge (10:39 a.m.)   42
Origin Story   43
You (5:55 a.m.)   44

❧

or   G   o   e   47

❧

Eve   59
Lion Child   61
The Good-Enough Mother   63
Travelers   64
The Mother & the Fish   66
Mom   67
What It Means   68
One Day a Mother   69
Root System   71
Another Thing No One Mentioned About Becoming a Mother 73
Lady of the Wood   75
Floating   76
North   78

❧

About the Author   81
About The Word Works   82
Other Word Works Books   83

To Leni & Benji

Earth is made from this alchemy of all children,
human and animal, combined
with our deep gratitude.

—*Mei-Mei Berssenbrugge*

And this child, this
window in my side,
boarded over all my life,
—how can I take the boards off, in this wind?

—*Jean Valentine*

She went missing

over a long period of time
a green hallway of years like
an ocean hung with tapestries you might

imagine a field sown with old buttons
and secret doors opening
to chimneys and roads and reflections

of stars in a piano the kind
that plays with no hands touching

the keys no one needed to make it

work and music filling the room once
you enter and close the air it's like nothing
you ever heard that music it's as if

everyone you ever left were singing

The Mother & the Girl

On one side the mother. On the other all
the animals around the girl. The girl who

will be a mother stands with all the animals
and raises a telescope to find the mother

and blot her out: a resounding animal cry
through the trees. The girl knows time

is running out and not like sand but like
words. The girl with a mother thinks about

blot versus *eclipse* versus *really getting
to know the enemy*. Under the eclipse the shape

of the mother. Under the mother the shape
of the girl in all the animals. The girl with

a mother eats as much of the mother as she
can stand to purge herself and become like

a shaft of light, clean and full of meaning.
On one side the mother, the side of paper

on which only the shadows of words appear.

Traveler

You are standing in an open field.
You said you would no longer believe
in signs until they come true, blue
sky not portent but blue sky, maps
the day you bought the boots less
important than their cracked tongues
and frayed laces. To the west, your
old red house. Nearby, a mailbox.
Open the mailbox. Another letter
from the land where you always
think you can live. You want advice
because you're setting out to make
the signs come true, stars laden
as bright horses. You will fall
in love again because you always
fall, but to the west, your old gray
house. Strike the match. No logical
system can capture all truths. Say
goodbye. No logical system is free
of inconsistency. Love is the memory
of a wooded lot before anyone knew
there were forests and distance was
the sound cicadas made at dusk.
You are standing in an open field.
Each time the first time, easy to say,
hard to keep moving. Be brave? You
stretch out and away like summer corn.

Home Movie

The castle is mostly given over to ghostly occupants
    —Angela Carter, "The Lady of the House of Love"

The titles roll and then the mother
sunning in the yard the look behind her eyes a clue to her
reliability but she's a good mother
she's just eaten the leaves her daughter brings her a clue
to surprise and maybe to absence
it begins when she asks her daughter what it means to kill
cue dark music cue dark sky
and they're in the brother's room the little boy they're tidying
his room and he's not there but
the father's there dear father the daughter doesn't
remember him speaking the daughter
guesses what it means to kill in an unclear season
in a blue room what it means to kill is
to take all the words from other people and watch them
disappear and they're dead for a long time
the daughter and brother and father they're happy sometimes
and dead all the time but before
the credits roll they've come back into hard-won lives
and finally there's a room full
of books cue a song and the mother's reading in dim light
cue a sad song and the title
of everything is how to come back from the dead

Beforetime

My parents knew I existed well
before I knew it myself. For years

they knew. My dad was a magician,
my mother a moth. We are all

refugees from the best hopes for
ourselves. What of you existed

before you remembered existing? Your
weight in their arms, the sound

of your voice? I didn't exist to myself,
but I had a smell, I drank and ate

what they offered: soft mornings,
the color of grass. No one else will

know that weight, the sound
of you then. In a castle everyone

called a house, we each built our own
small country. I was one kind

of animal, then I was another.

The Girl & the Mother

The girl with a mother throws the mother
to the ground as she runs, and
the mother becomes a mirror, the mother becomes
a forest. The mother flees to the opposite
side of the ocean, and the girl is free of the mother. The girl
celebrates the absence of mother before
the mother opens her mouth to reveal yard after yard
of silk teeth and inside the teeth, gifts: yarn,
homemade paper, railroad nail, matchboxes, blue glass,
tea. The girl plants trees in all the corners
of her house and considers routes constantly and wonders
about her own bright teeth. The girl
with a mother climbs into a tower to be free
of the mother, and the mother turns her sadness to a ladder
to climb to the girl and bring her back
to the banks of the river where she was born. The mother
gives up speaking to build a ship
out of ghosts, then touches the ghosts as if
they were sails—and the girl runs.

Birdsong

You crest the hill, light
a carnelian fire to let
the valley know you

miss it, even though
its stars were farther
away and the night

very cold. Above,
an invisible bird
makes the sound

of a ringtone with
its lungs and throat,
suggesting you are not

where you thought
you would be, setting
out. It's been days

since you spoke
to anyone, but days
exist less when

you're not speaking.
Like air you expand
to fill any space

and experience *lost*
as the impulse
to press something,

anything into wet
mud. With rocks
you construct a cell

tower to carry
these strange birds
through faucets and

radiators and teeth
to anyone who might
receive the signal and

think of you out here.

Coat of Arms

heraldic signs   a paper bag of lunch
my dad
stone skipped off the long tail of Alaska
Pensacola intercept
but hometown all along   packing our lunches
every morning

a bird stuck somewhere

my mom   homeless child
clothed and jumping into
the Holiday Inn pool   she kept a picture
cut from the newspaper of the Challenger
astronauts   all gone   pinned
to the wall

memory's fanfare and trumpets

an affair   did I know what that was
could I guess who with   these were questions
she really asked
in my five-year-old brother's room

that feeling in the pit of my stomach and
I didn't guess the right person and
then she was gone   off to Holland
and back

I told myself   both true
and not   I told myself
we were better off without her   no more
dust-mopping   vacuuming   buffing
those wood floors every day

she taught my brother and I to say
I love you in Dutch after the affair ended

it was around the time I was learning
about heraldry   asked to picture
my family's coat of arms

a row of apple trees stood at the back of our yard
yielding little fruit but apple trees   and
behind them railroad ties marking the end
of our yard   the beginning
of an empty lot   and I'd probably
paint my shield with
that lot   portal to the forest
it was waist-high in daisies
every summer

Thinking About Unrequited Love on a Train in Poland

White duck and white duck
reflection. Umber cow
in a green field. This is
a gray sky, this is a train

       window. I've hunted
       distance to outpace or
       hold tight to every feeling.
       You are coming, I tell

myself, an unreliable
narrator. I'm a breeze in a
blue curtain. The old story—
I threw down my mirror,

       it became a migration.
       Lifted the edge
       of my battlefield only
       to find your uniform's

stars and the way
the waters kept rising.
A baby animal is good
as any fresh start. I learned

       a long time ago
       to begin with a series
       of circles. One for
       the body, one for the head,

small circles for paws and
tail—and I was off. I never
saw you coming and by then
it was mutiny all over

again, my circumference
spent opening and closing
your voice. The only
thing left to say: I imagine

you happy just before morning,
and me, too!—sleeping with
the chance of all these miles
bringing you back.

Mother-Daughter

I visited her there somewhere
in the aughts. It was unclear
how I should respond to the trash and
overpass, silent waits
on stifling platforms. I wasn't helpful
to her and her addict, offering
him my own pills, sending money and
books, but this was after that, and she had
made a fresh start. We took the train
to Coney Island, and she was a deer
inside a souvenir shop while I was
a green boat on a bench looking out
at the water. My sleep-clothes were soaked through
each night. I'd attacked her adolescent skin
like my own then lost touch,
just late-night messages, a dream
of heart-to-hearts—
                        It's true I wanted
to know everything about her
once, nothing to be afraid of
in talking about dark matter,
childhood. But I had
a galaxy, so what did I really
know about it—stealing food, losing
brothers, a supposed escape? My North Brooklyn
days: I was in love with the empty
lots before any sign
of condominium—tall grass and
the Emerald City itself painted
onto a brick wall—
                        It was menopause,
and I missed the way my legs
once felt. I missed her—
                        I'm sure I did.

Mothers in *The Haunting of Hill House*

And then each year...she would be touched with the little
cold thought: I have let more time go by.
             —Shirley Jackson, *The Haunting of Hill House*

The mother pours poison into cups,
says *waking up* is staying together

forever, and she drifts in long green
silk. The mother says she will not

go back into the house at night, but
then she does. The mother has an affair

in Chicago that no one knows about
except the ghost of that wish raising

a glass in empty rooms. The mother
speaks like the Roaring Twenties and

appears out of nowhere again and again
with malignant intent. They're all

collapsed under the weight of the
feeling they once had about being

a mother. How it would be like a board
game box, how they would at all costs

maintain the illusion. The house in the
show is haunted, but it's just the mother

torn between mutually exclusive sighs.
The mother is always a suspect because

we've been taught from the beginning
not to trust a body that changes shape.

Level One

So bright and clear and pale in the afternoon
—Jolie Holland

One of two things will happen:
our avatar will live or it never
was. In the second case,
here's snow falling on a field
of snow. I'm forgetting the way

the village we left looked before all
I had was the memory of it growing
more improbable. For one, the fields.
A muted palette somewhere between
love and nonchalance, all the

monster blood turned pastel
as an antique carpet's faded
roses. Then the music. Your
theme song and mine were not
interchangeable, and the records

turned to throwing stars before
the tattered sails of my listening.
Turns out we heard the same thing
so differently. The programmers
worked all night to create these

illusions of proximity. Now
they draw you to me, but I'm not
here. When most alone, imagine
yourself in a montage of alone
others, hitting *start* repeatedly.

First the Mother

First the mother left then everyone
kept disappearing I fell in love
with windows from the outside fire

escapes landscapes I couldn't speak
passing outside trains transposing
their light into letters codes for

find me hidden in the long story
of my disappearance as daughter
my long alliance with men the quest

for a surrogate who would stay
even as I would go who would go
so I could lick absence like a flame

suture in reverie the edge of *me*
to the edge of *world* for who
would want to carry me no one

it seemed not across all conceivable
types of water not through all words
read aloud not beyond every form

of ceasing no one around then
but me in January still believing
in men deeper still in mothers

Violence & Magic

When you begin to think about
all the types of violence

facing small characters—a thorn
tucked into berries, iced walls,
apple-shine, the gun inside

a truck inside a shimmering city inside
the palm of someone's hand—it's less

a wonder that these stories
were ever for children than that
children could ever forget

their own strength.
                In the forest,
one thing leads to another without

question. Here I am, child again,
and my parents the illusion

of permanence. I kneel
here: their voices turned to water

by the long staircase, the opening chimes
of *M*A*S*H*, incense from hot toast
floating through the house. Thinking

of those nights now, I see the charm
was partly made by its breaking.

3D

I built my mother over the years, took her apart and
looked for the secret. She was a 3D printer, then
I was. I learned the distance between what I wanted
to be true. I studied the shape of lack and enough and
had the good sense to make others' mothers
my own. We made plans she cancelled, exchanged
data points until I lost the urge. Her need left no space
for anything else, and what I wanted to be true was
the snow-shadow in a room of lullabies, a requited
telephone. Recognizing my father as both
mother and father, I put away my tools, filled
myself with ink and meiosis to counter
my mother's lack with my life. Once I confused
absence with inheritance—then I stopped.

Unsent Letter from Philae, Comet 67P

*In February 2016, the European Space Agency announced that it
was unlikely that [the] Rosetta [orbiter] would ever pick up any
signals from [the] Philae [lander] again, partly due to failures in
a transmitter and a receiver on board.* —NASA Science

To approximate calligraphically the two hundred million miles
I traveled between your lungs to arrive so far from the sun, one

might sit before an empty jar of ink and imagine a distant white
rectangle like a field of snow not a single hoof or wheel

has impressed. It wasn't planned but of course I stopped near
a cliff, of course there was less charge than they'd hoped, and

there would never be enough time. If it was cold, I was calibrated
to say it but not feel it. If it was lonely, I didn't have a word

to say so. Together we carried twenty-one instruments. Stepping
out over the shoulder of South America, we disappeared into layers

of distance, and I wanted to tell you so many things even though
the dark also filled me with a vast quiet. We had no inkling of so

many things: the symmetry of a cat's stripes, morning glories still
in November, how patiently one of them waited for another to feel

what she felt. I knew what we knew, gravitational ellipses, then
what I could move through—frozen dust, methane, carbon dioxide,

ammonia—then I touched ground three times and lost you
to your orbit. In renderings, I am a small box moving away from you,

your wings outstretched against all those stars.

Rome

Before you, the idea of you,
crimson and secret. Seat of
appetite turned map, voices
of beasts bursting thoughts
into machines. But when
I arrived from all the other
countries, you were especially
light. Through rain at first,
then thrown open like tall
green shutters onto a golden
manuscript. It was the beginning
of the year that would change
me to a wolf, a garden. All
the light of my life poured
through the ceiling, one long
column from beginning to
this, dissolved into spaces
where any notion of me was
unencumbered as a drop
of air. Angels lifted roofs
on their fingertips and from
their bridges dreamed of time
and time while the angular
light of paintings repeated itself
across the city, marble light
spreading across the first days
of January. Epiphany. A gift
you might think lasts forever.

To the Body Inside My Body

A body is not a castle—it's a snowball,
        starting from very little. It stretches like a piece

of music around its listeners, forgets
        itself, carouses within a history of

devastation. When I say *body*, I mean *deep
breath*, but sometimes I also mean just look

at the model with dark bangs sheathed
        in blue menswear or the shape the blankets

make on a green park bench. We are not
        clean sheets of paper. A body is a zipper

from here to there, a spark, a flame
        breathed by chance winds into conflagration—

the scent of wood smoke years later
        bringing you back. A body repels, mends,

syncopates, loses. It's almost entirely
        six things: air, fossil, bomb, milk, glow,

falling. My mother says the body is
        a miracle, but it's not. A body happens

every day, the way death happens every
        day and is also not a miracle. You ask

what the body is and I can only say
        for sure *don't be surprised*. If it's a dotted

line on a map, you should know
        there's only one way to find out.

On Animals

The walls between the realms are so thin
—Chris Marker, *Sans Soleil*

I like rising quickly to feel
the dizzy birthright of anyone
foolish enough to persist
on two legs. We think we
aren't living like animals, but
see how we chew the news
like long grass, like we had all
the time in the world and nowhere
to be but here, our faces
turned down from the sky and
each other. The Romans knew
how a city can depend on its
geese and not the other way
around. The statue in Tokyo
for the dog and not the master
might be the culmination
of stone's search for something
true. Similarly, I keep hoping
my child will have a tail or
remain covered in soft fur, that
I'll love them as unfailingly as
the raccoons in the park. Like
an animal, I'll love them so much
I'll want to devour them—but
stop myself by saying words
instead and hoping these do
the trick. *Here's how to be
okay*, I'll say—the way we once
felt night and knew.

Lexicon

Is a baby more eyebrow or
suitcase   is it

a genie or a bowl of cereal   is it
more velvet or desert

a stick of butter or
a keening   but is it

a t-shirt or an ultimatum   is it more
winter or perfume

a fern or some gibberish
is it kiss or flag   but is it

more ruins or outboard motor
whiskey or shoes   is it

the exit or
the asymptote

a tango or some leaves
is it doorway or bath   but is it

more wood or weekend
an envelope or an eel

is it more flutes or
hide-&-seek

travails or fruit   but is it
willow bark or willow bark

a basket or in a basket
is it afloat or is it a flood

Reverie

On a day you were not
born I lost focus felt
three fish and

two fox tails at my
core pitched anvil after anvil
downtown and

skyward heard snow
falling at sea and also
dreamed myself

north held you in
a bubble in a lament and
escapade in

the relic of your name
pinned my eyes to light
across so

much cold air pinned
my mind to life mourned
my mind's

exile even as I celebrated
the sweet shape said
to the middle

distance *save me from
words* said to words *save me
from this*

body and no idea
none at all how you
would pull

the thread of me
tight into yourself gossamer
strand it

silvered light from
other bodies briefly back
into the field

The Tomboy & the Mother

Here of a night, my lungs will
fill enough to keep the machine
bodied. By day, the weight

of blood floats me like iron
floats, miraculously, some
say—but physics. I'm tired

especially of keeping myself
small, but I'm proud of keeping
myself small—and immense, too:

I never asked to be body on any
terms but my own. Once I felt
completely man and not mother,

but now I'm both at once, as once,
I'll say, it was the era of men
behaving badly on full view and

also a revival of drawing, whole
bodies and branches and cities
appearing astonishingly overnight

in several of our proudest institutions.

As If You Could Expect Anything at All

for Alex

There are events you prepare for in the abstract that change you
to a degree you could never anticipate. At the edge of Illinois,
where a river cuts the continent, this might have been tornado
or flood, maybe a blizzard, the shelves emptied of their wheat.

In New York City
during our short time
together *before*, we played
hooky for Midtown
coffees, saw rose-covered
wallpaper at the museum,
watched from roofs as the hand
of sunset pulled down night.

There's no way you can know you'll never do these exact things
again. This is where the house stood. Here's the line on another
century's brick to which the waters rose.

We ran through the world
one more time and missed
each other, forgot time,
found some animals—
the giant Snoopy on
Second Avenue, the bee,
a badger and fox and
little blue duck.

Looking back, one thing I see is how I'd carried my child-self for
the moment that was coming, waited a long time to be as a child
again with these children—and it would be hard letting go. In
Illinois, I was a child. My mother lived on the other side of the river.

We folded tiny clothes, clapped for
Hello, Dolly and *Julius Caesar*,
ordered one last pizza
at Angelo's.

And isn't it funny? We thought letting go was a one-time kind of thing. At least I did. Now in a room we could never have guessed, you close your eyes and listen to the sound of rushing water out the window.

Those Months You Were Afloat

I was not an explosion

I was not a harm to the infrastructure
not an intentional harm
to any creature

I was not a sip of pomegranate juice
with no nutritional value
but then I was

I was occasionally alarm but not all
the little lights massed like snow in the bar
across the street

I was a thumping inside but
not the green stem turning into a root
in a glass cylinder half-filled with water
near the window

I was not paper
pinned to a soft wall
not a mirror

I was
intricacies of architecture
hard flowers and spools of thread

I was an ongoing need
for ink and I was your foot
near my rib a little while longer
the way the steward tends
the kingdom when the king
is away

I was the kingdom

Castle

Once I was asked to write down all the ways
to use a stone and did not think of the castle,

though it may always have been thinking
of me, if our dwellings choose us as much

as our parents each other. The castle grew up
around me. I took my milk money and

paper bag of lunch from its counter every
morning and let myself in with a key

in the afternoon. My brother and I threaded
our limbs through those woods. The animals

hosted elaborate feasts on the grass. It was
painted gray by then, so I wrote that gray

place a note when we left and tucked it
into a crack in the attic. It took me years

to mourn our leaving (and its cause), though now
I know the body mourns even when we think

otherwise. If I'd known what I know, I might
have called stone *a thing to imagine myself*

into or *a thing by which to hold the passage
of time.* For years I kept many stones on my

desk to prove something about moving on and
what lasts, the places that hold us when

people let go. Seeing it now—clapboard saltbox,
drained moat—you'd never guess how much

richness it imparted to get me through.

Upon a Time

you're capsized
and just minutes
away the change
in scenery profile
shift an end
to transparency
you've been wave
and beat almost
invisible there
until now and quite
small a pip shaped
like a boat a bird
with iron sails
you've been a kind
of passive voice
alive but vague
now tadpole this
perpetual ocean
blood-filtered
light your smallest
room let these
go the first lesson
here being nothing
is yours for good

Drawbridge (10:39 a.m.)

for L

Even in extremis, note blue sky, branches,
   the cumulus safe, afloat. Even besieged,

breathe lemon verbena, how the prepositions
   blur: with/without, inside/outside, through/

through. Through lemon verbena, we
   arrived. Beyond lemon verbena, you and me.

You/me. Little fish, how I stood for days
   under water. How the sea swept the kitchen

floor. Me/you. Remember? The door closed
   between us, our own red door. The door fell

off its hinges to join the other myths, the others
   I also called myself—crystal mouse, cotton boll

and red seeds, holly charm and cloud charm, blue
   coin. Even when almost sunk and split, nearly

drowned and strung up and banished. The smell
   of lemon verbena, remember? I breathed and

you breathed and we slept in the torrent
   like coins at the bottom of a well. I wished

and never stop wishing and this is how I began
   rebuilding on the old site. Remembering for

both of us: you were inside and you were
   outside and I was with. I was without and

I was with. Once, my blood was
   in your hair. I like to think when the damp cloth

touched your forehead, it reminded you of home.

Origin Story

*A long pullback shot of some twelve hundred pairs of animals
entering the ark set a...record for processing hours: it would
have taken one computer more than thirty-eight years to build.*
—from a New Yorker *article on the making of* Noah

For each of my years, then: sixty or so
new animals and the mind containing

them the way a pocket contains
a magician's endless handkerchief,

red stuff pulled knot by knot into
thin air. Once I thought, *Have I*

*built in all these years a single memory
of land? Have I left anything holy*

alone? And my herds and flocks didn't
know but they also didn't care, so long as

stalls were mucked and hooves trimmed
like all the stories making up this place,

this city of mine in which the wilderness
comes and goes. My beasts. In pairs they

set about their work, and I mine, and
everything that came after was the story

not of me and not of journeys but of
the way small limbs move the air

as if to astound the very weather.

You (5:55 a.m.)

for B

The room where it happened was not—

If the event was an incontestable point, I approached from an opposite—

Time slowed.

Over and over again, I moved through it, the endless—

I was within time and I was not.

Every object vanished and the sounds and—

The room where it happened was the entirety of space folded into the shape of—

The usual dimensions ceased.

I was on one side of glass, dry and wet, standing up and lying hard on—

Water gave itself, water itself gave, itself gave water.

Time.

Over and over again, I moved through it, and time hollowed itself into—

In the room where it happened, dawn rang out.

I must have spent a thousand years having you.

Zork : The Great Underground Empire

an erasure

you are

                                                             all the windows

the trees

all the windows

you   lead into

a   winding   a
particular   edge

you are   nestled

you can see

a forest   sunlight

a   forest

a path

there is   ground
there is   darkness

47

                                              east and west

                                              a marvelous view

                        river
                  ramparts

                  a great dark

            for miles

                                        it is impossible for you to

shine

you are
                              a passage   seen
                                                              slightly a

glass

            attic   a

      knife

you are   living
lettering   nailed   to   a
                        door   a trophy
                              room

at your feet

you are   a   narrow passageway
          west   metal

     the   edge   of which cannot be seen
                    you are

          either   north or

                         a
different color

                    you might be

               a
bloodstain

                    a maze
                    a maze
                    a maze
                    a maze

                                        a skeleton
                              here

leather
          is
               part
                    of   passage

of

all
passages

you   come to
a   maze
you

are   small
locked

sunlight

leading up

a

scattered   staircase

this

circular

corridor   even

you

are

destroyed by

voices

you   can be heard

at the periphery
protecting

a white marble

                                    prayer   a

                            pillar

            a

pair of candles

                                    you

can

hear

a   rushing

in

the   earth

you
flow

north
to
the

center of the

chasm

there are "shores"

of jewels

you

    are

            impossible to cross

you are   a
      rising

hand

        of

water

           but

            behind

the water   is

        a
        glowing

         room

           a

      blue   doorway

you are

in the vicinity of

landing

running faster

along

cliffs

in darkness
you are   a   sandy

passage

a   cave

a

magnificent

room

there is an exit

leading

north

a square   mirror

and

small
  letters   etched in the rock

the entrance
is another exit

you are   strange
      you may   escape

this

heavy

    room
this
                      narrow

      bracelet

this

                                                mine

                                                        it might be

                        a   wooden ladder

                                        broken timbers

a
        small

                                                        machine
        reminiscent of a   face
                        the machine   is   open

you are standing

                                        close

                                                        to

                air

Eve

If I could just have
remembered carrying you,
I might have been
complete forever—
but I forgot, my
body forgot.

The muscle, I mean
the mind, so heavy
at first, beat chasing
beat and echoed together.

Anyone could see me,
but only I could know
the secret life of you:
undersea brush
of branches as if inside
a balloon, how
loneliness retreated
and fall arrived.

I knew everything just
by being—by sitting, sleeping,
drinking water, everything
that needed to unfold
was unfolding.

I mean everything
was holy.

If I could just
remember what I knew,
I might have it all again—
but there's no way
to remember how it felt,
evanescence.

Twice in my life, I was
half-man, half-beast,
and both parts were so gentle,
who would believe it?

Lion Child

after and with a line from H.D.'s "Circe"

It was easy enough to carry
a tree from one place
to another, and all the leaves and every
animal: owl, badger, red
fox, the deer and quick
rabbit—I carried them all.

A new apartment in summer,
leaves outside
the window just beginning
to play their shadows into our
rooms, warming
bricks, empty closets, bare
cupboards, summer spilling
us home.

And all of my sea-magic is for nought.

That year—
calibrating my body to
your hunger and following your voice
across the sea and back and
the park's lamps shining in the black
puddles come to float all
the oak, maple, ginkgo, plane, elm, willow,
and still more falling and all
they could hold.

It is easy enough to coax
a forest from the walls.
It is easy to spin
an impregnable orbit around
a name, to break,
it seems, but not to break, to follow
the soft padding of creatures

into an unknown sphere, stars
on every ceiling
under which you will sleep.

But tell me how to circle and
keep my hands circled around the light
while it widens like
winter steam to shine a world
that goes on and on, us,
then you,
then not even
you—

yes, a world.

The Good-Enough Mother

with a line from D. W. Winnicott

What's another word
for failure? I consider reclamation, restoration,
reassertion because I'm going
back to work on May Day, and you say
the mother must fail. But I won the race
against two bodies, was jetlagged
without going anywhere. I saw an entire flower, slept,
turned this body to food
and kept writing. The hardest thing I've ever done
came eighty-five days after
I pushed a human through a hall previously
no bigger than
a reed. My capacity for loss
is huge now. Show me yours?

What you call failure I call winning
myself back. Today I walked to the train and took it
downtown surrounded
by strangers. I showed up at work and did my job all day
cooking milk. *As time proceeds*
she adapts less and less completely, gradually,
according to the infant's growing
ability to deal with
her failure. But what's another word
for failure? What's another
word for a heart
smashed out and out beyond
any conception, any articulation, any cosmos—
just out and out?

Travelers

The mural on our little deck
in Montreal telescoped the start
and finish of civilization

as the artist saw it, Babel to 9/11
interspersed with figures of our
greatest good and evil, the extent

of our possibility. Aliens approach
from the masonic pyramid, its
gold the only color within

so much blue and gray, and their
banner proclaims or falsely
reassures or maybe mocks,

In God We Trust. This isn't
a poem about the mural, exactly,
but about you at one and a half

crouching in total absorption
to move fallen leaves and fragments
of leaves from gaps in the deck

to the hollow handle of a rubber
trashcan. How on a spectrum
of purity, it was so pure we

could barely take it. Bright pink
chairs, a stone Buddha near
the edge, and the day had gotten

so hot. Your little clothes
hung emptied of you when I
showered—cotton and salt—

their electric signal changing
the rhythm in my ribs,
again, to match your own.

The Mother & the Fish

*for Nicholas Hughes, with one line from Peter Linenthal
and two from Sylvia Plath*

Fish swim, the page tells my child and me, and I think about the rites
of those salmon you loved. Chinook and sockeye. Their movement

against the trawling current less explicable before you arrived—
evolution gone haywire some guessed. You thought it out

in banks and waves, all the silver Fairbanks had to offer. And
were you happy there for a while? Working clay on a wheel,

measuring flour and pecans in a snug house?

I look in and find no face but my own, your mother confesses. I think
about the succor you gave her, dear barn baby. I've now seen

for myself how the emptiness is held. But her terrible fish are not yours,
yours are the big ones far from shore. I close my eyes and they're pushing

their bodies again and again up the river, as if it were a single motion.
You found out it's smoothest where it seems most turbulent, but no fish

could fix the *smashed blue hills.* I know what it is to want that power.

Mom

I have two little ones now and now
see how you're my teenager and have
been all along. Asking for money to fix

the green car door that came to mysterious
harm. Never being there when I call. Gone
then suddenly returned, sending letters,

the same questions, gifts: homemade bird, a box
of choking hazards. Have you done your best?
Your staying alive must be at least part

of an answer, after childhood baths in Lake Erie,
six-cent popsicles costing three found
bottles, the empty rooms your brothers

left: silver box, green balloon. Once
you told me so much had gone wrong
at the same time—lost baby girl, dying brother—

and you'd just wanted to talk about it. Years
later when I ask about the possibility
of therapy, you say, *Why would I do that*

to myself? Here in the place of not knowing
what it might be to know you better,
I sieve fragments and shards, codes and

silences. You're a little girl in a rowboat with
your itinerant dad, somewhere in the 1950s. You're
twenty-something with hair longer than mine

will ever be, laughing with your green parakeet.
I keep you as close as I can because I love you
the way I might love someone else's child—

enough but never completely.

What It Means

because empathy is insufficient   could I unhook

my skin to become

another mother   could I peel back

my face to see with all the mothers'

eyes   my little boy asks what *white*

means   it's a color   I tell him   one

that repels all the other colors as if

they don't exist but that doesn't exist

without them   the forest

is burning everywhere we look   I hold

his small hand   his grown hand   a stranger

has come along a path and

put his hands around my little boy's

neck   I see flames and terror   a bird

flying away   the stranger squeezes

tighter and tighter   tighter   my little

boy asks what *mama* means   *Mama*

I say the one who arrived

at your name and

never left

One Day a Mother

One day a young mother
carrying her one-year-old
down subway stairs falls and

doesn't survive the falling.
Her baby is okay, but
the mind has already run

away, gravity and the terror
and everyone who happens
to be heading to work then,

and how do you go to work
then? One day a mother
doesn't look in time, and her

two-year-old is struck and
killed by an oncoming train.
Rush hour again, everyone

going home. The world is
barely made for us or we
for it. I live within the

illusion that as long as I'm
with you, you'll be okay.
Every day I hurry from

work to see you, to *prove*
you, and today I bring
an orange, whose juice

you love. The fruit is
my unkeepable promise
that everything will be

good. Here, sweet fruit—
and suddenly it's a palm-sized
planet you bite whole, tough

rind and all, not knowing
yet about waiting and
peeling. You jump into

these moments with every
particle of yourself,
heartbreaking trapeze artist,

and I watch, not knowing
what to wish myself
into: air or net or, yes!,

a clutch of notes from
the calliope, whose music
can be heard for nine miles.

Root System

It could be
that every generation
seeks to disprove
the proposition
that family will always
let you down—and
fails. But
I wrenched my arm
sleeping,
reaching out
for you as you fell
in my dream—
which also
says something
true.

Later, I lie
in bed and think,
I am, I am, I am,
not knowing
which of my minds
is doing
the thinking or
which of me
moves inside
the dream.

Every
mother is
an impossible
magic trick. See?
Once, twice,
I cut myself in half
and survived.

*

But I wonder what was it all for,
the having us, if she were
always going to disappear.
It's not that I stopped loving
but that the space between me and where
she was became, over time,
too great to cross.

*

Every child an impossible
magic trick.

See?

Another Thing No One Mentioned About Becoming a Mother

I enjoy finding so much hair
in my comb, the mother says. She
is tired, and she likes to eat cherries

at her desk. But what is hair
made of? she asks. Just
a filament of burned-out light,

fossil of me, a net for catching
soap and spit in the drain, my
signature. I let it down, the mother

says. I consider shearing but
resist so you'll recognize me. I tie
it back to do my work. When

there's a breeze, she rakes her
fingers through it, lets it float
away. She drinks coffee and

stretches her back. I'm afraid
to find so much hair in my comb,
the mother says. I'm afraid to stop

finding so much, its tentacles
winding all the sheets, the shoulders
of my dresses, and sometimes it finds

its way into our mouths. Sometimes
she feels the tickle of flies, but
it's just fallen strands. Who

will I be when there's no more
hair to lose? the mother asks. Like
moth wings, February, the dreaming

I woke to vanish, it's gone. I've
spun it all to milk, the mother
says. What remains protects

nothing but a person looking
less and less like me, those fears
so difficult now to remember.

Lady of the Wood

she is my mother
not a knight
but knowing quests
these are not
crows they dapple
every love
a seed of her
this present
the one place
she means
she comes back
not a bird at all
I made her kingdom
and loved the trees
seeing her in them
being seen
does a heart break

she went away
not an orphan
touching absence
diagnoses but
the pines here
of mine began as if
stretching toward
absence this is
I'll tell you what
the one place
she is my mother
I mourn again
my own
until I stopped
until she stopped
how many times
I'm still counting

Floating

We were strangers
nonetheless there we were again

this time at a make-up swim class
for our little ones a chance

encounter she from Sacramento but
I learned that later first it was

the baby in her hands another
December baby and was it

difficult having him I asked the way
new mothers like soldiers

can talk so comfortably about
bodies and how about yours

she asked her first was named
the same as my second our firsts

together in the water becoming
less afraid of floating and

out of the blue I said
it was a relief to find out my second

was a boy I was at home
with that energy she said

me too I was surrounded by
dad and brother energy as a child

I said me too my mom left
she said mine left when I was seven

I said mine left when I was ten
and there we were before parting

again the strangers we were
this time and she said

I just want to be *so present* for them
and I said yes completely

and I thought about it later
the mystery of it how we'd both

on a random Tuesday
been able to recognize ourselves

right there in the water

North

It's lucky how the snow fell
and then the cold that came to keep it
for five days so we could leave traces of ourselves and find
the broken orange sled still good enough
for sledding and smell the snow-specific smell
feel the snow-light when we woke
in dark rooms hear the quiet on that first morning
when we ventured into the world
like we had never seen it before I remember snow forts
as a child an olive-green ladle for scooping snow
I may have only ever made one
but like anything magic how much do you need
I remember white clouds
in a blue sky the morning we made it
to the hospital for L
snow on the ground in the park the morning before the long night
of B how we were chosen twice
in all the universe I remember driving north and alone
across Labrador and on the shoulder of Newfoundland seeing my first
and only iceberg floating down from the Arctic and
a man I spoke with briefly there
telling me how the polar bears ride them south then trek home again
how one came face to face with his dog one year
nose to the very nose
and the dog didn't start singing until the bear had seen
what she'd come to see and
turned toward whatever mystery it was
that called her back

About the Author

Rachel J. Bennett grew up on the Illinois-Iowa border and lives in New York City. Chapbook titles include *On Rand McNally's World* and *Game*, both from dancing girl press. Her poems have appeared in *Gigantic Sequins, LEVELER, Ninth Letter, Poetry Daily, Prelude, Rattle, Salt Hill, Sixth Finch, Smartish Pace, Sycamore Review*, and *Vinyl*, among other journals. She holds a B.A. in English from Grinnell College and has studied at Trinity College Dublin through the University of Iowa's Irish Writing Program and in Ecuador.

About The Word Works

Since its founding in 1974, The Word Works has steadily published volumes of contemporary poetry and presented public programs. Its imprints include The Washington Prize, The Tenth Gate Prize, The Hilary Tham Capital Collection, and International Editions.

Monthly, The Word Works offers free programs in its Café Muse Literary Salon. Starting in 2023, the winners of the Jacklyn Potter Young Poets Competition will be presented in the June Café Muse program.

As a 501(c)3 organization, The Word Works has received awards from the National Endowment for the Arts, the National Endowment for the Humanities, the D.C. Commission on the Arts & Humanities, the Witter Bynner Foundation, Poets & Writers, The Writer's Center, Bell Atlantic, the David G. Taft Foundation, and others, including many generous private patrons.

An archive of artistic and administrative materials in the Washington Writing Archive is housed in the George Washington University Gelman Library. The Word Works is a member of the Community of Literary Magazines and Presses.

wordworksbooks.org

Other Word Works Books

Annik Adey-Babinski, *Okay Cool No Smoking Love Pony*
Karren L. Alenier, *From the Belly: Poets Respond to Gerturude Stein's
    Tender Buttons (ed.) / Wandering on the Outside*
Emily August, *The Punishments Must Be a School*
Jennifer Barber, *The Sliding Boat Our Bodies Made*
Andrea Carter Brown, *September 12*
Willa Carroll, *Nerve Chorus*
Grace Cavalieri, *Creature Comforts / The Long Game: Poems Selected & New*
Abby Chew, *A Bear Approaches from the Sky*
Nadia Colburn, *The High Shelf*
Henry Crawford, *The Binary Planet*
Barbara Goldberg, *Berta Broadfoot and Pepin the Short
    / Breaking & Entering: New and Selected Poems*
Akua Lezli Hope, *Them Gone*
Michael Klein, *The Early Minutes of Without: Poems Selected & New*
Deborah Kuan, *Women on the Moon*
Frannie Lindsay, *If Mercy*
Elaine Magarrell, *The Madness of Chefs*
Chloe Martinez, *Ten Thousand Selves*
Marilyn McCabe, *Glass Factory*
JoAnne McFarland, *Identifying the Body*
Leslie McGrath, *Feminists Are Passing from Our Lives*
Kevin McLellan, *Ornitheology*
Ron Mohring, *The Boy Who Reads in the Trees*
A. Molotkov, *Future Symptoms*
Ann Pelletier, *Letter That Never*
W. T. Pfefferle, *My Coolest Shirt*
Ayaz Pirani, *Happy You Are Here*
Robert Sargent, *Aspects of a Southern Story / A Woman from Memphis*
Roger Smith, *Radiation Machine Gun Funk*
Jeddie Sophronius, *Love & Sambal*
Julia Story, *Spinster for Hire*
Barbara Ungar, After *Naming the Animals*
Cheryl Clark Vermeulen, *They Can Take It Out*
Julie Marie Wade, *Skirted*
Miles Waggener, *Superstition Freeway*
Fritz Ward, *Tsunami Diorama*
Camille-Yvette Welsch, *The Four Ugliest Children in Christendom*
Amber West, *Hen & God*
Maceo Whitaker, *Narco Farm*